Born in Burbage. 1922.

Mrs. Marion Godfrey,
29. Hrmove Court
Burbage.

Burbage
in old picture postcards

by Frank Shaw

European Library ZALTBOMMEL / THE NETHERLANDS

DEDICATED TO OUR NEW
GRAND-DAUGHTER – ABBIE TAY-
MON SHAW – BORN ON THE DAY
I COMPLETED THIS BOOK!

GB ISBN 90 288 6367 2

© 1996 European Library – Zaltbommel/The Netherlands

Introduction

The casual visitor to Burbage today will find it difficult – if not impossible – to find where Burbage ends and Hinckley begins. But there is no such problem to the south, where the boundary of Burbage, and indeed Leicestershire, is clearly defined as it has been for centuries by the A5 which is also the old Roman road called Watling Street. Originally the name was recorded as Burbach. John Nichols in his book 'The History and Antiquities of Aston Flamvile and Burbach' published in 1787 suggests that one source of the name would be 'Burr' (which was a form of thistle prevalent in the area) and 'Bach' (which is a small rivulet). Another possibility is 'Bur' (meaning a hill) and 'Bach' (meaning a spring). Since Burbage is on a pronounced hill and various springs exist this seems to be and is accepted as the more credible explanation.

Whatever the basis of the name it is first recorded in 1043 with the founding of the abbey of St. Mary in Coventry by Leofric of Mercia and his wife Gydgifu, more popularly known to us as Godiva. They endowed the abbey with about thirty manors, which included Burbage, Aston and Sketchley.

In 1100 these three manors were gifted to Robert de Flamvile, a Norman nobleman, by King Henry I (1100-1135) as a reward for the assistance he had given in a lawsuit. When Robert died the titles passed to his niece Erneburghe as his only heir. She married Hugh de Hastings who already held the manor of Barwell, and so Robert's name now only survives in the name of the nearby village of Aston Flamville.

The manorial title continued to be held by the Hastings family until about 1400 when, on the death of John de Hastings, it passed to Lord Reginald Grey of Ruthin. He was succeeded in 1441 by Edmund, who became Lord High Treasurer of England and was created Earl of Kent in 1465.

In 1639 Anthony Grey became the Earl of Kent, and also succeeded to the manor. He was the youngest son of a younger son and the last thing he had ever expected was that the titles would ever devolve upon him! He was a thorn in the side of authority because of his Puritan beliefs, but his influence seems to have kept Burbage out of any repercussions of the Civil War. He died on 9th November 1643. He had five sons and seven daughters, and there is a mural tablet in St. Catherine's Church in his memory.

Some years later, on 10th July 1682, Robert Cotes M.A. was born in Burbage. He was the son of a subsequent Rector but also directly related to Anthony Grey who was his great-grandfather! His grandmother, Grace Grey, was one of Anthony Grey's seven daughters. He became the first Professor of Astronomy at Cambridge but died at the age of only 34. He wrote the Introduction to Sir Isaac Newton's world famous work and Newton paid him the ultimate tribute on his early death: 'Had Cotes lived we might have known something.' His tomb is in Trinity College Cambridge.

Readers may like to know that Burbage also had its own 'Dads Army'! When the invasion of England by Napoleon became a serious threat early in the 19th century a meeting was held on 11th August 1803 when it was decided to form a Corps of Volunteer Infantry. In fact two companies were rapidly formed consisting of 120 men each. They covered the united parishes of Hinckley, Wykin, Burbage, Aston Flamville, Higham, Stoke, Dadlington, Sharnford and Sapcote. That was a good number of men in relation to the population, but in fact the numbers increased so that eventually four companies were formed. The cost of maintaining the Infantry was met by public subscription, and in 1808 they were officially named the West Leicestershire Regiment of Local Militia. By that time it numbered 841 NCO's and men.

Although the Local Militia were never to go into action, Burbage was still to have a direct connection with the Napoleonic Wars and in a famous battle at that. William Hands was born in Burbage in 1777 and joined the 90th Foot Regiment. By 1805 he was already Orderly to the General and stationed in the West Indies. On 4th June 1805 he was drafted as a Bombardier in the artillery and served on board Admiral Lord Nelson's flagship 'Victory' in the battle of Trafalgar. At the end of the war he returned to Burbage with a pension and became a frame-work-knitter. It must have seemed a very mundane existence after all his travels and excitement, but he lived to a good age and died in 1860 aged 83.

It is perhaps interesting at this stage to record the population levels of Burbage throughout this period. In 1377 the Poll Tax List showed the population at 100. For obvious reasons this figure could, however, be low! In 1004 (almost three hundred years earlier) the population was 125. By 1564 the Diocesan Return showed 285 inhabitants, and the Hearth Tax List of 1666 gave a population of 315. By 1801 it had risen to 1099 and by 1811 to 1348, 43 per cent of whom were employed in agriculture. In 1830 the population was 1504 and in 1840 it was 1608, still a very small population and with agriculture dominating. But the area was changing rapidly. By the end of the century there were already several factories established in Burbage dealing with hosiery and knitwear, as were the factories in Hinckley, Barwell and Earl Shilton. On 1st April 1937 Burbage and Sketchley became (very much against their will!) part of Hinckley Urban District and in the following month, on Coronation Day 1937, Burbage Woods, containing 50 acres of woodland, were handed over to the Council by the Rotary Club to be maintained as woodlands forever. In the same year Lady Lucas (Lady of the Manor) presented Burbage Common, containing 74 acres and adjoining Burbage Woods to the Council to be maintained as an open space forever. In 1948 George Ward presented 30 acres of land at Sheepy Wood to the Council. In 1956 Burbage Woods were listed as an area of Special Scientific Interest.

Just like Hinckley, Barwell and Earl Shilton, Burbage was enthusiastic in the fund-raising of the Second World War to the extent that it had a 'Burbage Spitfire'. But the Burbage Spitfire had by far the most illustrious pilot, the renowned Mungo Park. He led the Biggin Hill Wing in the Battle of Britain whilst Douglas Bader led its counterpart the Tangmere Wing. But there was to be a tragic end to both the Burbage Spitfire and Mungo Park, as both disappeared without trace on 27th June 1941 in an air-battle over St. Omer in Northern France.

The end of the Second World War in 1945 produced the actions that were to physically link Burbage and Hinckley. Development had been envisaged in the Council's Planning Report of 1944, and in 1949 and the early 1950's 133 acres of land were purchased. Included in this development was a 50 feet wide road connecting Rugby Road in the west to Burbage Road in the east. The 1000th post-war Council house was officially opened on 20th February 1953 on Sketchley Hill Estate. How times have changed even since then is best revealed by references to the Survey and Report on Burbage in 1950. That showed there were five drapery shops in Burbage, three cycle shops, four hairdressers and seven milk delivery rounds! There were three coal merchants, four undertakers, two bakeries, two cobblers and even one 'Corsetiere'! Finally, just to make your nostalgia operate in top gear, there were two regular policemen and twelve 'Specials'; and there were sixty buses each way (120 in total) each day between Hinckley and Burbage, and the fare was just one penny! How times change – and it seems not always for the better!

In conclusion I gratefully acknowledge the assistance of the Leicestershire Library Service at Hinckley with some of the photographs. But I must reserve a special 'thank you' for John McNaughton of Sapcote, who has provided the vast majority of the photographs from his wonderful collection, and given me the immeasureable benefit of his local knowledge. In meeting him I found a man with amazing knowledge of Burbage and a true friend indeed.

Frank Shaw

1   A delightful picture of
the Woodman's Cottage in
Burbage Woods in 1910.
The message on the reverse
is interesting: 'Dear Sarah, I
hope while you are in high
life you won't forget us
poor creatures at the Wood,
with love from Winnie.'

'FOXON'S SERIES.' WOODMAN'S COTTAGE BURBAGE WOODS.

2   Looking down Windsor Street to Lychgate Lane at the turn of the century. The first shop on the left is Wightman's, the shoe-makers. The Crown Inn, painted white, is further down the street, and The Bull's Head further along with four or five men and a small group of children gathered outside.

WINDSOR STREET. BURBAGE. NEAR HINCKLEY

3 Burbage Hall, built in the 17th century, which once belonged to the Earls of Gainsborough. Someone, who appears to be the butler, is with the two dogs on the seat in the centre.

4   Church Street looking north from its junction with The Horsepool. This photograph was taken in the early 1920's, because the newly-unveiled War Memorial is shown in the distance. The signboard on the right denotes The Anchor Inn where the Court Leat (a form of local government) was held. Each building is of quite different design, and yet the whole scene is one of tranquillity and charm. On the extreme right can be seen the Post Office with a shop on either side.

CHURCH STREET, BURBAGE, NEAR HINCKLEY

5   An open-air service in Burbage on 1st June 1919. It provides a classic opportunity to study the different styles of dress. The lady on the right seems to be having some trouble and is blissfully unaware of the photographer recording her concerns for posterity.

6   This photograph was taken in about 1910 and shows The Cross Keys Inn (opposite the churchyard) on the left. The inn remains as do the others in the same line, but the buildings jutting out are long gone. The village pump dominates the bottom of the picture and Crosslands Row (see photograph 18) appears on the far right in the distance. Note the long white aprons of the women crossing the road.

7   The Outwoods in 1909. The driveway to the house is now Elm Tree Drive, opposite the Brookside/Burbage Road junction.

THE OUTWOODS, HINCKLEY.

8   Len Ward, the delivery boy for Fosters Bakery, with their delivery vehicle for bread. Note the braking system on the rear wheel, the two buckets (presumably for food and water for the horse) at the driver's seat, and the sacks of wheat on the roof.

9   And here are some of the men who produced the bread! The date is unknown (probably 1945) but the photograph was taken outside the Co-op bakery in Church Street. Left to right: Len Ward, Herbert Foster, Alec Muir, Roy Dickson, Tom Shelton and George Ballard.

10   Church Street in 1930 showing Archers Cottage on the right, by the south entrance to the church. The cottage is named after George Archer, who purchased it in 1854 and was for many years Clerk to the parish council. Nearby was Burbage Town Hall where the Overseers of the Poor held their meetings.

CHURCH STREET, BURBAGE, NEAR HINCKLEY

11 Sketchley Grange in 1930 showing the old traditional form of 'haymaking' which has long disappeared.

12　The Simpson family provide a charming group with the family dog at Sketchley Fields Farm in July 1922. The property was demolished in 1936.

13　A close-up of the unveiling of Burbage War Memorial on 26th February 1921. The names of sixty men who died in the First World War are recorded. Less than seven years earlier they had set out with an innocent idealism never before seen in the history of warfare, only to see it crushed in the mud and squalor of Flanders. The memorial cost £400. The names of 31 men who died in the Second World War are also recorded. In September 1996 the names of 14 servicemen who were mistakenly missed off the monument or who had subsequently died were placed on a plaque on a rock in the Memorial Garden.

At the Unveiling of the War Memorial at Burbage, on Saturday, February 26th, 1921.

14   Nos. 1 to 9 Church Street, photographed from Lords Grocery Shop corner. The houses stood at the top of Lychgate Lane and were demolished in the 1960's to make way for the present Library.

15   Another fine view of Windsor Street – see also photograph 2. Behind the children on the left can be seen the sandstone pillars at the drive leading to the Wesley Chapel. Fosters Bakery stood where the house juts out in the centre of the picture.

Windsor Street, Burbage

16   A lovely view of Burbage Church which is dedicated to St. Catherine of Alexandria, and dates back to the 13th century. St. Catherine was martyred early in the 4th century by being tortured on a spiked wheel and then beheaded. She is commemorated each year (unknowingly) on 5th November by the 'Catherine-wheel' firework.

Burbage Church, Hinckley.

17   Burbage Mixed Church of England School in 1911 with Class 6 all looking like butter wouldn't melt in their mouths! Two of the boys wear the old-fashioned lace collar, but the rest wear the 'Eton' collar. The girls show greater variety, although almost all wear the pinafore apron. I do especially like the little girl third from the left in the row next to the front. She clearly knows how to pose for the camera!

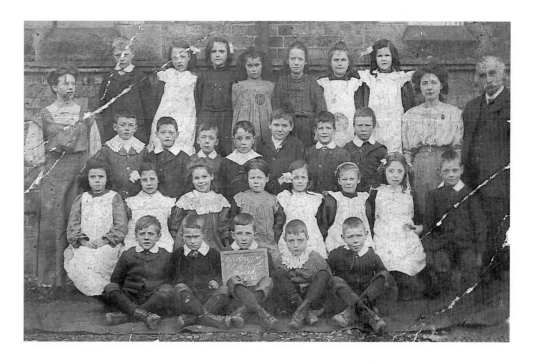

18   The interior of one of the cottages in Crosslands Row – see photograph 6. Crosslands Row was built between 1838 and 1841. The 1841 Census shows 14 dwellings in the row, two were empty, two housed agricultural workers and one housed an Irish school teacher. The other nine housed framework knitters. The photograph shows a typical kitchen area with a door leading directly to the coal store. A lead pipe hangs down the wall to the gas cooker and the only storage area is the two shelves on the right. The cottage was still occupied at this time – a cauliflower sits on the shelf above the two bags with other food items alongside it. The grinding poverty of this sort of accommodation is all too clear.

19 The cottages opposite Burbage Church Schools which were built about 1840 as cheap housing for framework knitters. These cottages also appear in photograph 6.

20   The village Wake Fair at Burbage at Whitsun in the early 1900's. It was held in the field at the top of Lychgate Lane.

21   The Blacksmith's near the top of Lychgate Lane in the late 1920's. Harold Holyoak is on the left, with Mr. Reeves fixing the shoe and Mr. Lisserman of Sharnford steadying the horse. The smithy closed in 1948 and Tilley's Garage stands on the site.

22   Sparrows Shop and Post Office at the junction of Windsor Street and Church Street at Wakes Week, in 1907. The children had come to watch the work of erecting roundabouts etc. The little girl standing with her mother in the doorway on the left is Edith Veasey, who died in 1991 aged 93. The whole block is still there and is recognisable, although the elevations have had major alterations.

23 Another view of Sparrows Shop. In the doorway on the right is Elizabeth Sparrow, the postmistress, who is also in photograph 22. Her father kept a butcher's shop in Windsor Street. In 1846 this building was The Boot Inn and the licensee at that time was Joanah Bond.

24   Church Street, St. Catherine's Church and Archers Cottage at the turn of the century. The building on the right-hand side is the old school, used before the National School was built in 1871. It was founded in 1825 by Countess De Grey, supported by subscription.

CHURCH ST. BURBAGE.

25   Cyril Swan of Lutterworth Road photographed in the 1920's. The lorry is a First World War Leyland he had purchased in 1920. It continued in use until 1936. A Swan lorry brought the choir stalls, Bishop's chair and panelling from Balliol College, Oxford, in 1937 for refitting in the parish church. Cyril Swan served as a special constable for many years and he was one of the strongest men in the area – he could easily lift an upright piano!

26   The Children's Procession at Burbage on Peace Day, 19th July 1919. The six ladies on the right make an interesting study.

27 The Lodge Houses to Burbage House photographed on 26th December 1904, when a record frost for the time was recorded. Later for many years they were unoccupied and – amazingly – there were serious proposals in the 1970's for demolition. I was with the Hinckley and Bosworth Council at the time and attended the meetings at which demolition was considered, opposing it vehemently. Demolition would have been an act of criminal folly, but thankfully we won the day and the houses have now both been fully restored.

28 The Wesley Chapel Sunday School class of 1909. Bearing in mind the lack of modern facilities and the poverty that was prevalent, don't they look amazingly prosperous, smart and alert?

29   The Sycamores Inn in Windsor Street, photographed in the early 1920's when it was still a private house owned by Mr. Parker Rice. Although the chimney heights have been reduced, the building is still recognisable with the entrance where the young man is leaning on the gate, now an entrance to the car park.

30 Newcombe's General Store in Windsor Street about 1908. Mr. Newcombe stands with the bicycle with the baby in the carrier, and the other man with the bicycle appears to be a rent collector or insurance agent from the collection bag on his handlebars. The baby is Mr. Newcom-be's son W.J. Newcombe, who later took over the business. The old factory is now Britannia Buildings, which was used as a Barracks in the Second World War. In the distance are the old cottages along Coventry Road.

31   A photograph taken in 1910 in Salem Road. Everyone has clearly put on their best outfit and the whole picture is one of a warm close-knit community.

32 A photograph in the early 1900's of Victoria Cottage, Coventry Road (formerly Potts Road), which was built in 1877. The cottage remains to this day almost unchanged.

33   A scene at the junction of Wolvey Road/Watling Street at the Three Pots in 1929. There were numerous accidents at this junction – there were no 'Stop' or 'Give Way' signs in those days – and so the only solution was the A.A. Patrol man in the picture, with his shelter erected between the two trees on the right. The name of the A.A. man is Jimmy Thomas. His motorcycle is parked on the left just across Wolvey Road and everything seems to be very quiet!

34   Sketchley Road in the early 1900's and what a contrast with what you would see today! The houses shown are still there, but the open land on the right that was Burbage Nurseries is now fully developed with houses to the extent that it is one continuous development all the way to Hinckley.

35   Grove Road in the
1930's looking towards the
church.

36   A real treasure is this photograph, taking us back to a history that every schoolchild was taught, the Crimean War of 1854 and the Indian Mutiny of 1857. Left to right Mr. Pratt, Mr. Robinson and Mr. Longham, all of Burbage and all of whom fought in one of these wars. Mr. Robinson in the centre has both campaign medals, but the date of the photograph is unknown and unfortunately no other information is available.

37   William Wheelock, the local brick and tile maker. His clay pit was in Lychgate Lane on the right-hand side, where the M69 now crosses the lane. His bricks were often used in 19th-century Burbage houses and his name appears on a brick in the Congregational Church together with another bearing the name of his wife, Edith Wheelock. This photograph was taken at the end of the 19th century.

38 A photograph of Thomas Seagrave Lord taken in about 1906. He was born in 1858 and died in 1915. His father, also Thomas Seagrave Lord, was the founder of the plumbing and decorating firm in 1831. In this photograph he is pictured with his daughter, Edith Elizabeth Lord. She subsequently married a Mr. Craythorne of The Anchor Inn, Church Street.

39 Burbage Cricket Club in 1911. Left to right, from the back: C. Hands, R.J. Clark, A. Smith, W.W. Dawson, W. Harding, J. Bailey, J. Robinson, J. Mawby, J.B. Perkins, J.P. Rice (captain), T. Turner, W. Hall and E.A. Rice.

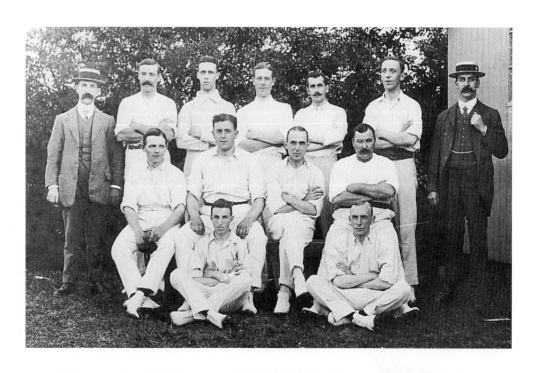

40   Grange Farm, Aston Lane, in 1911, and what a beautiful photograph this is! A date of 1608 appears inside the building and an extension at the rear bears the date 1697. The oriel windows contain the original glass and it was from The Grange that the first bus service from Burbage to Hinckley was started in the 1920's.

41   Another scene from the unveiling of the Burbage War Memorial on Saturday, 28th February 1921. A long line of widows, mothers, sisters and sweethearts are seated facing the memorial, each clutching a wreath of lilies in remembrance of a loved one. I wonder what individual thoughts each woman had, coupled with the pride, sorrow, and anger that must have been common to them all. Afterwards they each planted a small wooden cross in the loose ground at the base of the memorial.

At the Unveiling of the War Memorial at Burbage, on Saturday, February 26th, 1921.

42   The conclusion of the unveiling ceremony at the War Memorial and this time it is the men whom we can study. Young and old, but all solemn and dignified, each must be remembering a son, brother, comrade or acquaintance who had made the ultimate sacrifice. The raw anguish is still on each face as it was across the country at similar ceremonies.

43　Reverend Fletcher receiving his mail from Mr. Oliver, the postman, outside The Rectory. The photograph was taken prior to the First World War. Before it became The Rectory the house was called Moat House, from the dry moat which is still visible from Grove Road.

44 The only known photograph taken inside the Rectory, it shows four of the oldest residents of Burbage at a supper in their honour in 1945. Miss Ada Pughe and the Rector, the Reverend R.D.H. Pughe, stand at the back. Seated, left to right, are Mrs. Bishop, Mrs. Randle, Mr. Reuben Smith and Mrs. Wood.

45 Church Street about 1914 looking down towards The Horsepool. Although most of these properties have suffered from the rendering over of the brickwork, the elevations, roof lines and chimneys are virtually unchanged. The house on the left in the sunlight is now the current Post Office.

46   The Burbage Cooperative Society Central Premises and Offices in Church Street in 1930. Established in 1874 the first Secretary was Jeremiah Robinson and there were three branch shops in Burbage. These were at Three Pots Estate, Sketchley Road and Windsor Road.

47   Burbage Village Green at the turn of the century. This became the site of the Burbage War Memorial – see photographs 41 and 42 – that followed the carnage of the First World War. But in this photograph that horrific future could never have been contemplated. Children play on the Green and two old men talk as they had all done for so many years. A pony and trap waits patiently outside a house and, for a few more years, all was well in the world...

48   Rose Carrigan standing in the doorway of John R. Carrigan, tobacconist, in Church Street with 'J.R.' standing behind the bicycle. The shop was established in 1891 and this photograph was taken in about 1920. Charles Carrigan is seen on the extreme right. The shop was situated just below The Anchor Inn and the metal sign on the right advertises Lucky Star cigarettes at six for one penny! Quite apart from the cost of six cigarettes for ½ new pence, the very idea of a metal plate bearing a fixed and stated price is indicative of the level of financial stability of that period.

49   Apart from the loss of the iron railings and the rendering over of the brick-work, these houses at the junction of Church Street and The Horsepool are little changed. This photograph was taken about 1900 and also shows the Congregational Chapel of 1895, which still stands but has had major changes to its front elevation.

50   A wedding party on 4th June 1907 near The Croft, The Horsepool. Miss Mayne, the midwife – see photograph 69, is seated front left, next to the groom and his bride. Front row: nurse Mayne (later Mrs. Gent), May Dudley, Tom Haygarth, Annie Haygarth, Mrs. Sarah Mayne and Elsie Dudley. Middle row: Elsie Dudley, Eleanor Mayne, Kate Mayne (later Mrs. Dudley), Ada Baum (later Mrs. Lord), Alice Mayne, ?, Florrie Mayne, ?, ?. Back row: ?, Edgar Mayne, ? and Mrs. Emma Botterill.

51   A lovely study of an old lady and two children, who are probably her grandchildren. The pram is a wonderful example of the Victorian period and do note the knee high boots of the little girl. All we know is that the cottage was in the lower area of Church Street about 50 yards from the junction with Lychgate Lane. It appears on the left of photograph 14.

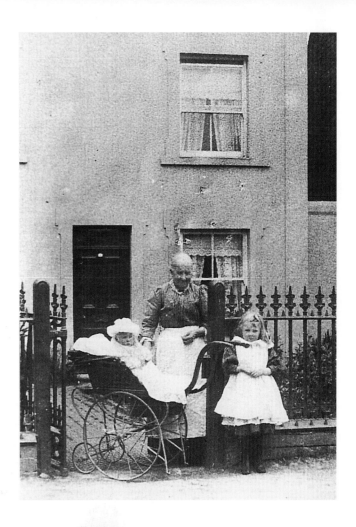

52   The Cottage Farm in Lychgate Lane photographed in 1898.

53   Lychgate Lane. The footpath next to the gas-lamp on the left is now the entrance to Woodstock Close.

54   Burbage Road looking towards Burbage at the turn of the century. The area is totally rural in character with just three ladies on the left-hand footpath and Mr. Chesterman's fully-laden coach and horses on its way out of Burbage. It could carry twelve on top and six inside. The photograph was probably taken in what is now the Elmtree Drive area.

55 The Toll House which stood at the bottom of Cock Hill, now called the Burbage Turn. It is where the Burbage Road and Sapcote Road meet. The baby girl in the arms of the lady became Mrs. Spencer of Barrie Road, Hinckley, and I met her when producing the first book 'Hinckley in Old Picture Postcards'. In 1759 the tolls were two shillings (10 new pence) for the hire of two horses, 10p (4 new pence) for corn and hay for two horses, and 2p (1 new pence) for the toll for two horses.

56   Sunny Hill, off For-
resters Road, photographed
in the 1920's.

57 A V-E Day Party in 1945 in Hinckley Road and although everyone was hoping to have a super time some of the children look somewhat apprehensive! The lady on the left holding the young child is Nora Payne, who still lives in Hinckley Road! She was the wife of Ron Payne, the well-known Burbage ventriloquist. The lad front right is Fred Connolly, who still lives in Burbage.

58   A photograph taken outside the Church of England School some time before the Great War. It shows a large Yorkshire-type wagon which had a tight turning circle because of the small front wheels which turned underneath the wagon. The precise location of the photograph, opposite the Cross Keys Inn, can be seen better in photograph 6.

59   A view down Hinckley Road from outside the Church of England school in about 1910. Crosslands Cottages are on the right (see photographs 6 and 18). The boundary wall of the Church School can also be seen on the right.

60   A typical example of a hosiery factory in the 1920's. This photograph was taken in the Iway Hosiery premises situated between what is now Sunnydene Garage and the Church Hall, in 1928. In the photograph, front row: Florrie Chamberlain, Doris Colledge, Mable Tansey, ?. Middle row: Flossie Goodwin, Florrie Fisher, Lily Burton and Elsie Goodwin. Back row: Elma Farmer, Mabel Chamberlain, John Iliffe, Arthur Greenway, Eileen Greenway, Doris Greenway, Laura Bennett and Dola Kay.

61   June 1923 and a celebration of the Golden Jubilee of Burbage Co-operative Society. In the background is the junction with Grove Road, from which the procession was heading to the Infant's School in Hinckley Road for tea.

62   A lovely photograph of the restoration work to the Church Tower of St. Catherine's in 1912. The clock which can be seen behind the scaffolding – with faces to the north and south walls of the tower – was provided to commemorate the Golden Jubilee of Queen Victoria in 1887.

63   Burbage Parish Church bells before being recast in 1925. The bells date from 1701 to 1761 and the children of the Church School were photographed on this historic occasion with their Headmaster, Charles Higham, and the Rector, Reverend R.D.H. Pughe.

64 A fine view of Church Street and St. Catherine's. The large house on the left is said to have been occupied by George Canning, one time Prime Minister, who died in 1827. The tree surrounded by railings is the Victorian Jubilee Tree of 1887, which was destroyed by a gale on 29th March 1952. The roadsweeper has left his wheel barrow on the left – he appears to be going to meet the pony and trap passing the church, but he could be heading for The Cross Keys Inn!

65   Another photograph of the same area with the Victoria Jubilee Tree on the extreme right. This picture would have been taken about 1925. The car belongs to Mr. P.E. Brightmore and he records: 'It cost me £12-10-0 (£12.50) taxed and in running order.'

66   Lutterworth Road in the 1920's from the Chequers Inn.

Lutterworth Road, Burbage. No. 2878.

67   Another photograph of Sketchley Road – see also photograph 34 – taken about 1910.

68   A photograph of George Archer, who was for many years Parish Clerk. Archer Cottage next to St. Catherine's is named after him. He acquired it in 1854.

69 Nurse Louisa Mayne, who was the first trained and qualified midwife in Burbage. She qualified on 22nd February 1906 and in the period 1906-1931 she delivered over 1,000 babies. Her fee was 2 guineas (£2.10) for a confinement and 12-day visiting. She covered the area of Aston Flamville, Smockington, Sketchley and Burton Hastings, which was a huge area if you consider she had to turn out in all weathers at all times with nothing but a pushbike. She appears in the family wedding photograph number 50.

70   Jemima Leason, who lived in Loomes Square which is now the Liberal Club car park. In the photograph – taken by Nurse Mayne – she is collecting sticks in her apron for the fire.

71   A 1910 photograph of the cottages at the rear of the War Memorial which was then a village green. Even in those hard days doesn't this picture epitomise a prosperous tranquillity? Note the thatched cottages on the far right that adjoined the Co-operative Buildings in Church Street.

72　Church Street in 1910 looking toward The Horse-pool. The thatched cottages on the right are a real gem. What a tragedy they are no longer there!

73   The lower part of Church Street and the entrance to The Horsepool at the turn of the century. The shops on the right are now private houses and Chestnut Villa had not yet been built next to Horsepool House in the centre. A lovely wide expanse of quiet open road is shown, with St. Catherine's Church spire in the distance.

74   The Horsepool around 1910. This is the only house still standing out of those erected in this area at the turn of the century. Madge Campton (later Mrs. Owen) is on the left with Mrs. Emma Botterill, who lived at the house. The small boy is Stanley Campton.

75 Burbage Church of England School and St. Catherine's photographed in about 1900.

76   Grove Road School in 1928 and the gardening class demonstrate their prowess! Notice that the two boys on the left and one in the back row are wearing 'flat caps' so fashionable with older men at the time. Left to right, front row: I. Bamford, G. Parker, V. Davies, H. Fisher, A. Goodwin, K. Foxon and S. Hill. Centre row: H. Cooke, C. Baum, R. Brandrick, J. Brown, Mr. Charles Higham (Headmaster), D. Medhurst and A. Dowell. Back row: F. Garner, A. Malin and H. Letts.